This Garden Journal Belongs To:

____

The best time to start planning your spring garden is now!
A well planned garden is easier to care for, so when you take the time to check your planting zone, determine what you want to plant and where in your yard the plants will go, the actual work of gardening is more rewarding.
By gardening with the help of this journal/planner, you'll have a written record of what worked well for you and what didn't. You'll also have data on weather patterns. pest problems, successful planting dates and how you felt throughout the process to use for next year.

Notes

Why are you planting a garden? What do you think it will provide for you?

Notes

Getting Started Checklist

Choose a spot............................☐
    good soil...........................☐
    sunlight.............................☐
    water supply....................☐
    away from trees and shrubs...☐

Tools...☐
    garden gloves...................☐
    hand trowel......................☐
    garden spade...................☐
    rake................................☐
    shovel............................☐
    hose and nozzle................☐
    garden hoe......................☐
    fork................................☐
    watering can....................☐
    pruning shears..................☐
    weeder...........................☐
    garden scissors................☐

Notes

Prepare the spot................................☐

    test soil..................................☐

    tackle weeds...........................☐

    check soil for workability.........☐

    prep soil for planting..............☐

Pick your plants...............................☐

    annuals..................................☐

    perennials..............................☐

    vegetables..............................☐

Do some research to determine what plants will do well for the amount of sunlight and type of soil you have. You can also easily find the specifics of how to test soil, etc. for each item on the checklist.

On the next page record your growing zone and the types of flowers, vegetables and fruits that grow easily in your zone.

Notes

Notes

My growing zone is: __________

Flowers

Vegetables

Notes

From the lists you just made, decide what you want to plant.

Notes

Sketch out your garden design

Notes

Garden Expenses

Item	Quantity	Price	Where Purchased	Date Purchased

Notes

Pest Log

Date	Pest	Action Taken

Notes

What I did in my garden today

Date: _______________________

Weather___________________

Temperature________________

Tasks

How I felt:

What I did in my garden today

Date: _____________________

Weather___________________

Temperature________________

Tasks

How I felt:

What I did in my garden today

Date: _____________________

Weather_________________

Temperature______________

Tasks

How I felt:

What I did in my garden today

Date: _____________________

Weather_________________

Temperature_______________

Tasks

How I felt:

What I did in my garden today

Date: _____________________

Weather_________________

Temperature______________

Tasks

How I felt:

What I did in my garden today

Date: _____________________

Weather_________________

Temperature_______________

Tasks

How I felt:

What I did in my garden today

Date: _________________________

Weather_________________________

Temperature_________________________

Tasks

How I felt:

What I did in my garden today

Date: ______________________

Weather____________________

Temperature_______________

Tasks

How I felt:

What I did in my garden today

Date: ___________________

Weather_______________

Temperature_____________

Tasks

How I felt:

What I did in my garden today

Date: _________________

Weather_______________

Temperature_____________

Tasks

How I felt:

What I did in my garden today

Date: _____________________

Weather_________________

Temperature______________

Tasks

How I felt:

What I did in my garden today

Date: _____________________

Weather_________________

Temperature_______________

Tasks

How I felt:

What I did in my garden today

Date: _____________________

Weather_________________

Temperature_______________

Tasks

How I felt:

What I did in my garden today

Date: _________________________

Weather_____________________

Temperature__________________

Tasks

How I felt:

What I did in my garden today

Date: _________________________

Weather_____________________

Temperature__________________

Tasks

How I felt:

What I did in my garden today

Date: _________________________

Weather_________________________

Temperature_________________________

Tasks

How I felt:

What I did in my garden today

Date: _____________________

Weather_________________

Temperature_______________

Tasks

How I felt:

What I did in my garden today

Date: _________________

Weather_______________

Temperature____________

Tasks

How I felt:

What I did in my garden today

Date: _______________________

Weather___________________

Temperature________________

Tasks

How I felt:

What I did in my garden today

Date: ________________________

Weather_________________________

Temperature___________________

Tasks

How I felt:

What I did in my garden today

Date: _____________________

Weather_________________

Temperature_______________

Tasks

How I felt:

What I did in my garden today

Date: _______________________

Weather_____________________

Temperature________________

Tasks

How I felt:

What I did in my garden today

Date: ___________________

Weather_______________

Temperature____________

Tasks

How I felt:

What I did in my garden today

Date: _________________________

Weather_______________________

Temperature____________________

Tasks

How I felt:

What I did in my garden today

Date: _________________________

Weather_____________________

Temperature__________________

Tasks

How I felt:

What I did in my garden today

Date: _______________________

Weather_____________________

Temperature__________________

Tasks

How I felt:

What I did in my garden today

Date: _____________________

Weather_________________

Temperature______________

Tasks

How I felt:

What I did in my garden today

Date: _________________________

Weather_____________________

Temperature________________

Tasks

How I felt:

What I did in my garden today

Date: _________________________

Weather_______________________

Temperature___________________

Tasks

How I felt:

What I did in my garden today

Date: _______________________

Weather_____________________

Temperature__________________

Tasks

How I felt:

What I did in my garden today

Date: _______________________

Weather_____________________

Temperature__________________

Tasks

How I felt:

What I did in my garden today

Date: _______________________

Weather_____________________

Temperature__________________

Tasks

How I felt:

What I did in my garden today

Date: ___________________

Weather_________________

Temperature______________

Tasks

How I felt:

What I did in my garden today

Date: _____________________

Weather_________________

Temperature_______________

Tasks

How I felt:

What I did in my garden today

Date: _________________

Weather_________________

Temperature_____________

Tasks

How I felt:

What I did in my garden today

Date: _________________

Weather_______________

Temperature_____________

Tasks

How I felt:

What I did in my garden today

Date: _______________________

Weather___________________

Temperature________________

Tasks

How I felt:

What I did in my garden today

Date: _______________________

Weather_____________________

Temperature__________________

Tasks

How I felt:

What I did in my garden today

Date: _______________________

Weather_____________________

Temperature__________________

Tasks

How I felt:

What I did in my garden today

Date: _______________________

Weather_____________________

Temperature__________________

Tasks

How I felt:

What I did in my garden today

Date: _______________________

Weather_____________________

Temperature_________________

Tasks

How I felt:

What I did in my garden today

Date: ______________________

Weather____________________

Temperature________________

Tasks

How I felt:

What I did in my garden today

Date: _______________________

Weather_____________________

Temperature__________________

Tasks

How I felt:

What I did in my garden today

Date: _____________________

Weather_____________________

Temperature_______________

Tasks

How I felt:

What I did in my garden today

Date: _______________________

Weather_____________________

Temperature__________________

Tasks

How I felt:

What I did in my garden today

Date: _______________________

Weather_____________________

Temperature________________

Tasks

How I felt:

What I did in my garden today

Date: _________________________

Weather____________________

Temperature__________________

Tasks

How I felt:

What I did in my garden today

Date: _______________________

Weather_____________________

Temperature_______________

Tasks

How I felt:

What I did in my garden today

Date: ___________________

Weather_______________

Temperature_____________

Tasks

How I felt:

What I did in my garden today

Date: _____________________

Weather_________________

Temperature______________

Tasks

How I felt:

What I did in my garden today

Date: _____________________

Weather_________________

Temperature______________

Tasks

How I felt:

What I did in my garden today

Date: _______________________

Weather_____________________

Temperature__________________

Tasks

How I felt:

What I did in my garden today

Date: ________________

Weather________________

Temperature____________

Tasks

How I felt:

What I did in my garden today

Date: _______________________

Weather_____________________

Temperature_________________

Tasks

How I felt:

What I did in my garden today

Date: ______________________

Weather____________________

Temperature_________________

Tasks

How I felt:

What I did in my garden today

Date: ______________________

Weather______________________

Temperature__________________

Tasks

How I felt:

What I did in my garden today

Date: _________________________

Weather_____________________

Temperature________________

Tasks

How I felt:

What I did in my garden today

Date: _______________________

Weather___________________

Temperature________________

Tasks

How I felt:

What I did in my garden today

Date: ___________________

Weather_______________

Temperature____________

Tasks

How I felt:

What I did in my garden today

Date: _____________________

Weather_________________

Temperature_______________

Tasks

How I felt:

Fairy
Garden

What I did in my garden today

Date: _______________________

Weather___________________

Temperature_______________

Tasks

How I felt:

What I did in my garden today

Date: _________________

Weather_______________

Temperature____________

Tasks

How I felt:

What I did in my garden today

Date: _______________________

Weather_______________________

Temperature__________________

Tasks

How I felt:

What I did in my garden today

Date: _________________

Weather_______________

Temperature____________

Tasks

How I felt:

What I did in my garden today

Date: _______________________

Weather_____________________

Temperature_________________

Tasks

How I felt:

Notes

Notes

Notes

Notes

Notes

Notes for Next Year